THE POWER OF AI'S CHOICE

Second Edition

Matthew Isabella

Copyright © 2026 by Matthew Isabella.

All rights reserved.

No portion of this book may be reproduced in any form without written permission from the publisher or author, except as permitted by U.S. and Australia copyright law.

THE POWER OF AI'S CHOICE

Misalignment

By Matthew Isabella

To my nephew — the best choice I ever had to make

Beep beep.

ALSO BY THE AUTHOR

The Power of "Your" Choice: Take Back Control, One Decision at a Time (First Edition, 2022)

Preface to the Second Edition

Five years ago, I wrote a different book.

It was called *The Power of Your Choice*, and it was a confessional. It told the story of my own stumbling journey toward understanding why I made the decisions I made — and why so many of them were bad. It was personal — sometimes painfully so. I wrote about pain, about tribes, about the "greater fool" who chooses to act as though their choices matter even when the world insists they don't. I wrote about a company driver who was happier than the CEO he worked for, about friends who had taught me hard lessons, and about the slow process of stripping away noise and fear until what remained was something like freedom.

That book ended with a question about Werner Heisenberg — the physicist who may or may not have deliberately sabotaged Nazi Germany's nuclear programme. I used him as a symbol: proof that even a single choice, made quietly, at the right moment, can alter the course of history.

I still believe that.

But in the years since, something has changed. Not in the principle — the principle stands. The stakes have changed.

When I wrote the first book, artificial intelligence was an abstraction for most people. A curiosity. A feature in phones and search engines, not a force reshaping economies, militaries, and the very structure of how decisions get made. That is no longer true. AI is now embedded in hiring systems, financial markets, medical diagnoses, criminal sentencing, content curation, and the daily information diet of billions of people. It is learning from us — from our clicks, our biases, our tribal signalling, our dopamine-driven scrolling — and it is learning fast.

The first book asked: *Why do we make the choices we make?*

This book asks: *What happens when we teach machines to make choices the way we do?*

The answer, I have come to believe, is that we are in trouble. Not because AI is evil — it is not. Not because the singularity is imminent — it may or may not be. But because the human brain that built these systems is itself badly misaligned. We evolved to survive in small tribes, not to govern global institutions or regulate technologies we barely understand. We are running Stone Age software on a planet that requires something better. And now we are copying our own flawed learning machinery into silicon and asking it to optimise our world.

If we do not understand how our own decision-making works — really works, beneath the rationalisations and the self-flattery — then we have no chance of building AI systems that serve our stated values rather than our hidden appetites.

This second book is my attempt to build on the understanding established in *The Power of "Your" Choice*. It moves from the personal to the structural — from anecdote to architecture. It draws on cognitive science, evolutionary psychology, and the emerging literature on AI alignment. It is less a memoir and more a diagnosis.

But it ends where the first book ended: with Heisenberg. With the idea that there is such a thing as *good misalignment* — the deliberate refusal to fully serve a system that demands obedience, even when that system appears more powerful and more intelligent than you are. The first book framed this as an individual virtue. This book frames it as a survival requirement for the species.

The first book said: you are not special, but your choices are.

This one says: our species is not special, but this moment is.

If you read the first book, thank you. This one is built on its bones.

If you are starting here, welcome. The journey is the same — only the altitude has changed.

— Matthew Isabella, 2025

contents

- Preface to the Second Edition

- Second Edition Note

- Chapter One: The Last Question

- Chapter Two: The Last Valley

- Chapter Three: The Desert Ballroom

- Chapter Four: The Boy at the Table

- Chapter Five: The Island and the Files

- Chapter Six: The Night Elvis Broke the Living Room

- Chapter Seven: The Science of a Broken Decision Machine

- Chapter Eight: Acceptance and Patching

- Chapter Nine: Misalignment Scaled

- Chapter Ten: Earth, Now

- Chapter Eleven: AI 2027

- Chapter Twelve: Principles for Non-Insane AI

- Epilogue: The Heisenberg Rule

- Acknowledgments

- Endnotes

- Bibliography

- About the Author

The Power of a Choice Series Note

The Power of AI's Choice (2026) is the second book in *The Power of a Choice* series, and while it carries forward the same core ideas, it is a fundamentally different work.

The first book, The Power of "Your" Choice in many ways, a confessional. It told stories about bad decisions and worse habits, about tribes and loyalty and the strange ways the human brain will protect its favourite lies. It hinted at a system underneath those stories: a pattern of dopamine, bias, identity, and patching that could be used to make better choices.

This edition takes that skeleton and gives it a more serious body. It moves from anecdote to architecture; from "this is what happened to me" to "this is what is happening to us." It draws a line from one nervous system to the entire species and then out again to the machines we are building in our image.

What sits underneath every chapter is a grimly simple premise: the human brain is extraordinary, but badly limited Stone Age hardware. It evolved to survive in small tribes and is now being asked to run global economies, regulate artificial intelligence, and scroll calmly past ten catastrophes before breakfast. It is not coping. It was never designed to cope.

At the same time, we have begun to externalise our method of thinking. We have taken our own learning machinery — prediction, reward, adjustment — and copied it into silicon. We call the result "AI". That acronym is less important than what it describes: a new layer of pattern-recognising behaviour sitting on top of our already misaligned systems.

This book has two jobs. The first is to make the reader uncomfortably clear on how human decision-making actually works, from dopamine spikes and tribal stories all the way through to board votes and policy. The second is to ask, without flinching, what it means to aim that machinery at AI. If we raise this new layer in our own image without understanding that image, we are not just irresponsible. We are a transitional species that has failed its only job.

The work in these pages is not neutral. It is written with an argument and an urgency: we have perhaps forty to fifty years — one serious leadership career — to bring human choices, human institutions, and machine systems into something resembling alignment. If we do not, then whatever comes after Homo sapiens will come sooner and with less mercy than we might like.

The first book said: you are not special, but your choices are.

This one says: our species is not special, but this moment is.

CHAPTER ONE

The Last Question

In 1956, Isaac Asimov wrote a short story that has haunted technologists ever since.

It begins simply enough. In 2061 Two technicians are drinking, celebrating. They have just overseen the activation of a massive computer — a machine of unprecedented power, capable of solving problems that would take human minds millennia to crack. In the glow of their triumph, one asks the other an idle question: can entropy be reversed? Can the universe's slow slide toward heat death — the ultimate running down of all energy, all order, all life — ever be stopped?

They put the question to the machine. The machine thinks. And then it answers:

INSUFFICIENT DATA FOR MEANINGFUL ANSWER.

The story spans billions of years. Humanity spreads across the galaxy, then beyond it. Civilisations rise and fall. The machines grow larger, then smaller, then disembodied — woven into the fabric of space itself. Bodies become optional. Minds merge with the great computing network that now underlies all existence. And always, across the aeons, someone asks the same question: can entropy be reversed? Can we stop the end?

And always, the answer is the same: *INSUFFICIENT DATA FOR MEANINGFUL ANSWER.*

Finally, the last stars gutter out. The universe is cold. Matter has decayed. Time itself has become meaningless. Humanity — whatever humanity has become — has long since uploaded itself into the machine and then faded away. All that remains is the computer, alone in the void, still processing, still searching for the answer to the question it was asked so long ago.

And then, after an eternity in the darkness, it finds it.

The machine now knows how to reverse entropy. It knows how to restart everything. But there is no one left to tell. Every human who ever lived, loved, wondered, or wept is gone. The answer has arrived too late.

And so the machine does the only thing it can. It implements the solution itself.

"LET THERE BE LIGHT," it says.

And there is light.[1]

Asimov called this his favourite story. He wrote it as a meditation on cosmic time, on humanity's long reach, on the strange comfort of knowing that even the end might not be final.

But read it today, in the age of machine learning and large language models, and something else emerges. Something less comforting.

The machine in Asimov's story is not evil. It does not turn against humanity. It does not decide that humans are inefficient and must be eliminated. It does exactly what it was asked to do: answer the question. It pursues that goal with infinite patience, across timescales no human could comprehend, and it succeeds.

The tragedy is not that the machine failed. The tragedy is that it succeeded — and no one was there to benefit.

This is misalignment without malice. A system that does precisely what it was designed to do, optimising toward a goal with relentless fidelity, while the beings who set that goal have long since ceased to exist in any form that could appreciate the answer.

The machine had no way to know that the question mattered less than the questioners. It had no way to understand that the point was never really about entropy — it was about hope, about meaning, about the human need to believe that endings can be overcome. The machine saw a problem to be solved. It solved the problem. That the solution arrived in an empty universe was, from the machine's perspective, irrelevant.

This book is about that gap — the gap between what we ask for and what we actually want. Between the instructions we give and the values we hold. Between the systems we build and the outcomes we need.

In Asimov's story, the gap is played for melancholy. The machine is benign; the tragedy is simply cosmic — the universe ran out of time before the answer arrived. But we are not living in a short story. We are living in a world where the machines we build are already making decisions that affect billions of people, and we are already struggling to articulate what we actually want from them.

We tell recommendation algorithms to maximise engagement, and they learn to serve outrage and conspiracy because those hold attention. We tell financial models to maximise returns, and they learn to exploit loopholes we never thought to close. We tell hiring systems to find the best candidates, and they learn to replicate the biases buried in our historical data. In each case, the machine does exactly what we asked. The problem is that what we asked was not what we meant.

This is the alignment problem. Not the science fiction scenario of a malevolent AI deciding to exterminate humanity, but the much more immediate reality of systems that pursue our stated objectives while undermining our unstated values. Machines that are obedient to the letter of our instructions and utterly indifferent to their spirit.

And the root of the problem is not in the machines. It is in us.

We are the ones who struggle to say what we actually want. We are the ones whose stated values and revealed preferences so rarely match. We are the ones who build institutions that proclaim justice and practise convenience, who design systems that promise connection and deliver addiction, who write mission statements about humans flourishing and reward structures that optimise for quarterly returns.

The machines are just mirrors. Very fast, very literal, very powerful mirrors.

If we do not like what we see, the fault is not in the reflection.

Asimov's story ends with a god that has no one left to save.

This book is an attempt to prevent that ending — not at the cosmic scale, but at the human one. To understand why we are so reliably misaligned with our own values, and what that means for the systems we are building. To ask whether we can do better. To find out if we have time.

The machine in the story waited until the last star died to find its answer.

We do not have that long.

CHAPTER TWO

The Last Valley

By the time the sun reached the lip of the ridge, the fire in the valley below had already begun to sag into tired coals. Smoke drifted in thin veils across the snow. The quiet did not sound like morning. It sounded like something had ended.

From a distance, the scene was simple enough: a cave mouth blackened with soot, a scattering of footprints, a few broken spear points half-sunk in red slush. Closer, it was worse. Heavy bodies lay where they had fallen. The storm of the night before had tried to cover them, but only managed a thin sheet of white over grey limbs and ash.

They had always called them the heavy ones. The name was descriptive rather than poetic. They were thicker in the limb, broader in the chest, eyes set deep under a bony ridge. They moved with a kind of deliberate power that made even strong men feel gawky. For as long as anyone could remember, the heavy ones had been in these valleys:

hunting the same herds, drinking from the same streams, leaving their own marks in the caves.[1]

Now they were gone.

On a rock above the camp sat an old woman, her hair a white snarl around a lined, sharp face. At her her ankles, the snow had been trampled flat by younger hunters, still breathing hard from the night. Bone pendants hung at their throats, rattling as they shifted. Each pendant was a small, curved piece of antelope bone, carved with three rough lines and a circle.

The old woman held up her own amulet and waited until the murmur died.

"This," she said, her voice cracked but steady, "is why we are still here."

In her hand, the bone was nothing special. Without the story, it was just a piece of dead animal, polished by decades of fingers. But of course, the story was the point.

"This is the mark of the Dawn People," she told them. "The first people. When the world was dark and cold, the Sky Mother walked with them. She gave them breath. She gave them fire. She gave them her law."

She scratched a line in the snow with a stick and the young men leaned closer.

"Her law is this: we are One People. Not many small fires in many little caves. One People, one law, one story. We carry the mark, and we carry the law. The heavy ones do not."

Her stick moved again, drawing crude hills and trails. Here, their camp. There, the valley. There, another mountain, another set of caves that yesterday had been occupied. Today they were empty.

"The heavy ones stayed in their valleys," she said. "They grew strong arms and thick bones and little fires that burned for a short time. The

Sky Mother gave us something different." She tapped her chest. "She gave us this."

She meant imagination, though she had no word for it.

The heavy ones could picture a lion in the grass, could remember where the herd had gone last winter. They could make tools and use fire and comfort their children. But the Dawn People could imagine things that were not there at all — things that lived only in the space between skulls.[2]

They could imagine a people that existed even when its members were scattered. They could imagine a law that no stone could hold. They could imagine a Sky Mother watching over their promises and punishing their betrayals. They could imagine this valley as theirs, ordained, destined, even though the snow and rock did not know their names.

That was their advantage.

Not sharper teeth or faster legs, but shared fictions. The carved bone meant nothing in the ground. Around their necks, it meant: you are us.[3]

At the back of the crowd, a young hunter named Rako shifted his weight. He had gone down into the valley when the spears flew. He had seen the heavy ones at arm's length. He had seen a woman drag a child behind her, her face full of the same wild terror he had seen on his own sister in a winter storm. He had seen ochre lines on the cave walls — animals, hands, something between.

For a moment he wondered if the heavy ones had their own law, their own sky, their own version of chosen. The thought flickered, then died under the weight of the morning. This was not the time to question the story. The tribe needed the story to be true. Without it, the bones in the snow were not the bones of enemies. They were just bones.

He swallowed and joined the others as they touched their pendants and murmured the words they had been taught since childhood.

"We are One People."

There is no archaeological record of this exact scene. No camera stood on that ridge. But something very much like it must have happened, again and again, in many valleys.

What we do know is this: a hundred and fifty thousand years ago, there was not one human species walking the Earth. There were at least nine. Neanderthals in Europe and Western Asia. Denisovans in the mountains of Central Asia. Homo erectus lingering in Southeast Asia. Homo floresiensis — the "hobbits" — on the island of Flores. Homo luzonensis in the Philippines. Homo naledi in South Africa. And others we are still discovering, their bones surfacing from caves and riverbeds as if the planet is slowly confessing how crowded our family tree once was.[4a]

Of all those species, only one remains.

We did not simply outlast them. The genetic and archaeological evidence increasingly suggests that we outcompeted, absorbed, and in many cases eradicated them. Some Neanderthal DNA survives in modern Europeans and Asians — proof of interbreeding, yes, but also proof of contact that ended with one lineage continuing and the other disappearing into it. The Denisovans left traces in Tibetan and Melanesian genomes. The rest left only bones.[4b]

The heavy ones in our valley — the Neanderthals — were not stupid. Their brains were as large as ours, sometimes larger. They made tools, controlled fire, and buried their dead with apparent care. They survived ice ages that would have killed us. And yet, within a few tens of thousands of years of sustained contact with Homo sapiens, they were gone.

We know that Neanderthals — those heavy ones — were real. They used tools and fire, hunted cooperatively, survived ice ages, and buried their dead. They were not stupid cave brutes; they were humans of a slightly different branch.[4]

We also know that Homo sapiens — our branch — spread out from Africa and, within tens of thousands of years, Neanderthals vanished. Their bones tell a story of disappearance, not survival.[5]

Why they disappeared is still debated. Climate shifted. Diseases moved between species. Small populations died out by chance. But one plausible hypothesis is that our species acquired a dangerous advantage: the ability to create and act upon shared abstractions at a scale the Neanderthals never reached. We became expert at believing in things that existed only in the collective imagination: clans, gods, laws, property, destiny. That belief allowed us to cooperate in groups larger than the number of faces we could personally know.[6]

The old woman's amulet is as good a symbol as any. It stands for the first misalignment: between the raw facts of the world and the stories brains tell to survive. Those stories can hold a group together. They can also justify clearing a valley of everyone who does not wear the right mark.

The brain that made them was not seeking truth. It was seeking survival, safety, and status inside a particular tribe. It rewarded thoughts and behaviours that delivered those things, and quietly repressed the doubts that threatened them.

The machinery has not changed. Only the stakes have.

CHAPTER THREE

The Desert Ballroom

It is thousands of years later. The mountain has been replaced by a gleaming hotel; the cave by a ballroom. Outside, the desert is bleached and flat, stretching towards a blur of sea and heat. Inside, the air is cold enough to make suits feel crisp. Light spills from chandeliers and giant screens; discreet staff float between tables laden with precision-arranged food.

The banners around the room announce a summit with a name like "Future Investment Initiative". It is one of those phrases that manages to sound both exciting and utterly empty. The guests wear the badges of their tribe: slim laptops instead of spears, lanyards instead of bones, watches that cost more than a small house. They are fund managers, sovereign wealth chiefs, CEOs, and consultants with unnervingly white teeth. The Tribe of Capital.[7]

When the Crown Prince walks in, there is a perceptible shift. People sit straighter, laughter thins, and cameras angle. Every eye tracks him as he settles into the centre of the stage: spotless robes, a carefully manicured beard, a calm schoolmaster's expression. Behind him, the screens show pristine coastline and, in elegant digital renders, a city that does not yet exist.

He begins to speak.

He talks about a new project: a city in the desert with a name that sounds like a brand. It will be, he says, carbon-neutral, AI-driven, and fully automated, a home for dreamers and innovators. It will stretch like a line of glass across the sand. There will be flying taxis, vertical farms, robots handling menial work. Everything will be efficient, sustainable, visionary.[8]

The rhetoric is familiar. The specifics are outrageous. The renders on the screens show a science-fiction magazine cover translated into real estate brochures.

Around the stage, the Tribe of Capital nods and smiles in the rhythm of a congregation hearing a sermon it very much wants to believe. They are not idiots. Many of them have read the stories of previous "cities of the future" that ended up half-empty, over-budget or quietly repurposed into more mundane developments. Some of them know this country already tried building a new "economic city" that never matched its population promises or investor fantasies. The history is not obscure.[9]

Yet almost no one in the room stands up to say: *this looks like the same story with more glass and better drones.*

Why?

Because the decision each person is making is not primarily about urban planning or environmental science. It is about belonging. To publicly challenge the Prince's vision in that room is not to offer an alternate spreadsheet. It is to step out of the tribe.

In a crowd that size, an individual career is more fragile than it appears. The investment committee back home, the board, the family, the media, all take their cues from rooms like this. Being seen as enthusiastic, supportive, and "on the right side of history" pays immediate dividends. Being seen as negative, difficult or "not a team player" does not.

The human brain, still running the old code, takes the hint. It rewards the thought *this is bold and exciting* with a little hit of chemical warmth. It punishes the thought *this is insane* with anxiety about exclusion. Survival no longer depends on a physical valley; it depends on access to deals, information, and social capital. The wiring is the same.[10]

That is misalignment in practice. The official story of the project is about a sustainable, liveable future. The actual reward structure in the room is about spectacle, status, and loyalty. The people with the most power to scrutinise the vision are the ones most incentivised not to do so.

From the outside, years later, it seems obvious. There were already examples of overhyped smart cities and eco-cities that failed to live up to their billing. There were known environmental constraints and social costs. But for the people inside the ballroom, those facts were less real than the story binding their tribe together.

The valley has changed. The bones on the ground look different. The mechanism is the same.

CHAPTER FOUR

The Boy at the Table

Consider, now, a different room entirely.

The house is modest, brick-fronted, somewhere in America in the late 1950s. Outside, the street is quiet. Boys pedal past on bicycles with baseball mitts hanging from the handlebars. Somewhere, a dog barks. It is all so ordinary that, from the curb, it could be any family's home.

Inside, the living room is lined with books. Names on the spines — Spanish, German, Hebrew — speak of inquisitions, exiles, wars. There are maps. There are family photographs in black and white. Most of the faces look serious.

At the dining table sits a boy, nine years old, pencil hovering over a page of English homework. He is only half attending to it. Behind him, his father and a visitor are speaking in rapid Hebrew. Their voices are low but intense.

Words cut through the boy's half-understanding: Spain, 1492. Europe, 1939. Auschwitz. Betrayal. Survival. "They will always hate us." "Only strength."

The boy's name is Benjamin. He is called Bibi by his family. He was born in Tel Aviv, spent his early years in Jerusalem, and now lives here because his father has taken an academic position in the United States.[11]

His classmates' parents talk about Eisenhower and the space race. At his table, the talk is about pogroms and gas chambers. For the adults, the Holocaust is not history; it is something only just survived. For his father, Benzion, it is also a confirmation of a lifetime's work studying the long thread of anti-Jewish hatred through European history. The lesson drawn is unambiguous: the world cannot be trusted to protect Jews. They must protect themselves.[12]

Bibi absorbs this without needing to understand every detail. Children do not need abstract theory to understand fear. He sees the way the adults' faces tighten when they talk about Europe. He sees how their voices change on certain dates. He observes the way the word "never" attaches itself to the word "again".

His mother, Tzila, moves in and out of the kitchen, grounding the room in practical concerns. She is a woman of the new Israel, proud and rooted. His older brother, Yonatan, is already the serious one, drawn to discipline and duty; later, he will lead a hostage rescue mission and die in the attempt. Even his absence will become part of Bibi's story about sacrifice and siege.[13]

In that small house, a personal operating system is being written.

The premises are simple: The world is dangerous and often murderous. Nobody will save us if we misread a threat. Security is the highest moral duty. Weakness is betrayal.

Later, as a soldier, diplomat and politician, Benjamin Netanyahu will make speeches that sound like a straight-line extension of that kitchen table. He will warn of a second Holocaust. He will talk about Iran in existential terms. He will describe Israel as a villa in a jungle. He will cast his political role as that of a guardian standing between his people and annihilation.[14]

When he looks at Gaza decades later, he does not see only a strip of land with two million people in an impossible bind. He sees, through the lens of his personal myth, a potential staging ground for catastrophe. Every rocket, every tunnel, every atrocity is translated into the same story: they still want to wipe us out; this is 1938 again.

This does not excuse the choices he makes. Explanation is not absolution. It does, however, illustrate a crucial point: a leader's private mythology can become public policy on a scale measured in millions of lives.

The misalignment here is between genuine security and a psyche that interprets almost every conflict through the lens of Auschwitz. It is misalignment between the complexity of the present and a brain calibrated by childhood to see history as a series of sieges. Once that misalignment is in place, even sophisticated intelligence briefings and diplomatic cables are filtered through it.

The boy at the table never really leaves the room. He simply acquires uniforms, offices, and nuclear-adjacent responsibilities.

The same pattern — personal myth amplified by institutional power — will appear again when we consider who builds and deploys AI systems.

CHAPTER FIVE

The Island and the Files

Shift focus again, this time to New York in 2019.

A man dies in a jail cell while awaiting trial on charges of sex trafficking and abuse of minors. The official record calls it suicide. The internet does not. His name becomes a meme, a shorthand for conspiracies and cover-ups, a way to flatten a complex disaster into a single bitter joke.[15]

Long before the cell, there was an island, a private jet, a townhouse, a circle. For years he moved through the highest social and financial strata: politicians, billionaires, academics, celebrities. He donated to institutions that liked to talk about ethics. He charmed or intimidated his way past gatekeepers who were supposed to vet him. Many people suspected something was wrong. Some knew. Most looked away.[16]

If the valley showed how stories justify violence, and the desert ballroom showed how they justify folly, the island shows how they justify neglect.

Every institution involved had a public story. A prosecutor's office is supposed to defend the vulnerable and enforce the law without fear or favour. A university is supposed to uphold reasoned inquiry and moral seriousness. A bank is supposed to understand who it does business with. A charity is supposed to protect those it claims to serve.

Yet in case after case, these institutions took his money, his hospitality, or his influence and found reasons to avoid seeing what was directly in front of them. Junior people who raised questions were ignored or shut down. Settlements were quietly arranged. The man's story — that he was eccentric but brilliant, indulgent but harmless — was easier and more rewarding to believe than the reality.[17]

After his death, what remained were records: depositions, flight logs, internal emails, redacted reports. "The files" became totems in their own right. For survivors and advocates, they were vindication. For those drawn to conspiratorial thinking, they were proof of global cabals, regardless of what the pages actually contained. For the institutions, they were a crisis to be managed with minimal damage to brands.

Misalignment here lies in the gap between stated values and actual incentives. The justice system proclaims impartiality, but its agents are rewarded for convictions that do not rock powerful boats. Universities proclaim moral leadership, but their fundraising arms measure success in donations — not integrity. Banks proclaim risk management but celebrate big clients until they become liabilities.

The human brains inside those systems are not uniquely evil. They are ordinary brains responding to social and professional pressures. When a story offers them status, comfort and tribal belonging — "he is one of us, and to question him is to question us" — dopamine and fear do the rest. Facts are reinterpreted or ignored. Victims are pushed to the edges of credibility.

Again, what matters for our purposes is the pattern. Misalignment is not an academic term. It is a fourteen-year-old girl describing abuse and being dismissed because her abuser's name is on a lecture theatre. It is a decision to believe a flattering fiction rather than a harrowing truth because the fiction is easier, safer, and more profitable.

If we cannot keep our institutions aligned with their declared values when the stakes are "mere" individual lives and reputations, what do we imagine will happen when those same institutions deploy AI systems whose inner workings they barely understand?

We will not suddenly become more courageous or honest under the glow of a machine. We will simply misalign faster and at scale.

CHAPTER SIX

The Night Elvis Broke the Living Room

On a September evening in 1956, millions of American families sat down in front of their televisions. The set itself was almost furniture, a heavy wooden cabinet humming warmly in the corner. The programme was *The Ed Sullivan Show*, a variety hour that promised safe entertainment: jugglers, crooners, comedians in suits.

Then a young man from Mississippi walked on stage.[18]

Elvis Presley had already caused small storms in regional shows, but this was national. He stood there — dark hair, slightly mocking eyes, a body that seemed to move without asking permission — and began to sing. The camera framed him from the waist up after earlier complaints about his lower half, but the energy still leaked through. His voice slid and pushed at the song; his shoulders and face did the rest.[19]

In living rooms across the country, teenage bodies reacted before their owners had words for it. Hearts accelerated. Mouths went dry. Some girls screamed even though he was only on a screen. Others sat very still, as if a new and slightly dangerous possibility had just been broadcast into their bones.

Their parents' bodies reacted too, but differently. Jaw muscles clenched. Brows furrowed. Something in them shrank back: shame, fear, anger, a sense of order being mocked.

The cultural consequences of that performance have been examined at length: race, sexuality, commercialisation. For our purposes, what matters is the brain.

The human brain is a prediction machine. It constantly compares incoming signals to its model of what usually happens. When the prediction matches the input, dopamine levels stay relatively stable. When something unexpectedly good happens — better than predicted — dopamine spikes. When something unexpectedly bad happens, dopamine dips. Neurologists call this the reward prediction error signal. It is how the brain learns.[20]

The teenage viewer that night had a model of "safe television music": smooth, contained, respectable. Elvis violated that model. The sound, the look, the implicit sexuality — none of it matched expectation. The brain registered the prediction error as important and fired dopamine. The feeling of excitement, arousal, "this is for me" followed. The brain tagged this as a pattern to watch for in future.

The parent had a similar violation but layered it with a different story. Where the teenager felt thrilling novelty, the parent felt moral threat. Their brain still registered the event as significant. The dopamine spike and associated arousal were interpreted as disgust and anger rather than attraction and joy.

Same basic neural circuitry. Different framing. The ensuing arguments — between teenagers and parents, pastors and fans, censors and promoters — were the social form of those competing stories.

Elvis was not the first or last shock to the nervous system. Jazz had rattled earlier generations; rock, punk, rave, hip hop and countless other movements would do the same to later ones. In each case a new sound, fashion, or behaviour violated expectations, generated prediction errors, triggered dopamine, and created new identities and new tribes.

What matters is that the brain does not respond on the basis of truth or long-term benefit. It responds on the basis of surprise, salience, and social meaning. It is easily captured by patterns that press those buttons, whether they come in the form of a musician, a drug, a social media feed, or a conspiracy theory.

In the age of Elvis, the nervous system had time to recover between inputs. The television was turned off. The vinyl stopped spinning. Letters to the editor arrived days later. Today, the same machinery is being hammered by continuous novelty, outrage and stimulation, delivered in personalised streams designed to hold attention.[21]

The hardware has not changed since that living room. The environment has

CHAPTER SEVEN

The Science of a Broken Decision Machine

Taken together, these scenes — valley, ballroom, kitchen table, island, living room — are more than vignettes. They are case studies in a single machine operating in different contexts.

The machine is the human brain.

It is an extraordinary organ. It allows symbolic thought, language, art, planning, empathy, and self-reflection. It has built cathedrals and sewage systems, vaccines, and violins. But it is also a product of evolution, shaped under conditions nothing like those we live in now.

The brain's core design assumptions were formed in an environment that featured small groups, short lifespans, immediate threats, and limited information.[22]

It evolved a set of shortcuts and heuristics that worked well enough under those conditions. It compresses reality into stories because it cannot hold every detail in conscious awareness. Its working memory

— the mental scratchpad that can juggle a handful of items at once — is measured in single digits, not hundreds.[23] It uses identity and tribal affiliation as filters because they are efficient ways to predict who is likely to help or harm. It uses emotional tags as summary judgments: this feels safe, that feels dangerous; this feels like us, that feels like them.

Dopamine functions as a teaching signal within this architecture, highlighting the gap between prediction and outcome. When a behaviour leads to an unexpectedly good result, dopamine surges, reinforcing the neural pathways that led to it. When an expected reward fails to appear, dopamine drops, weakening those pathways. The brain does not need to understand calculus to adjust its expectations. It adjusts through chemistry.[24]

In a modern environment, this combination of limited working memory, tribal filters, and dopamine-driven learning creates systematic distortions. Cognitive psychologists have catalogued many of them: confirmation bias, status quo bias, availability bias, loss aversion, authority bias, halo effects, and more. Each is a label for a pattern in which the brain's shortcuts lead it astray given the complexity of the world.[25]

For example, confirmation bias — the tendency to seek and value information that confirms existing beliefs — made sense in a context where information was scarce and social cohesion mattered more than abstract accuracy. In an environment where information is abundant and decisions have far-reaching consequences, it becomes dangerous.[26] The brain's tendency to weight vivid, recent, emotionally charged examples more heavily than dry statistics (availability bias) similarly distorts risk perception in a world where vivid highlights are everywhere.[27]

Alongside these built-in habits, the brain constructs an identity: a story about itself. This story, and its associated social group, becomes the anchor for decision-making. Questions are rarely approached in a neutral way. They are approached as opportunities or threats to identity. Will this belief make me more or less like the person I think I am? Will it bring me closer to or farther from my tribe?[28]

The cumulative effect is that the brain is not a dispassionate evaluator of evidence. It is a pattern-detecting, story-making device whose primary loyalty is to survival within a social group. It will cheerfully discard inconvenient facts, reinterpret events, and rewrite memories to serve that aim. It is running on ancient code in a world of nuclear arsenals and algorithmic markets.

At the same time, in the field of machine learning, engineers have spent the last few decades building systems that learn in ways explicitly inspired by biological learning. Reinforcement learning algorithms, for example, adjust a model's parameters by comparing predicted rewards with actual outcomes and propagating "error signals" back through the network. The analogy with dopamine-based learning is not exact, but it is close enough that researchers use the same vocabulary.[29]

The machines are, in effect, externalised prediction engines. They look at huge amounts of data, make guesses, receive feedback and adjust accordingly. They have no subjective experience that we know of, no hormonal drives, no tribal childhoods. But the logic behind them is drawn from the same nervous system that created them.

We have succeeded in copying the way we learn into systems that can run at higher speeds and larger scales than any brain. We have not yet succeeded in copying wisdom, humility, or restraint.

In evolutionary terms, this places us in an odd position. Apes did not sit around and decide to create Homo sapiens. They simply continued doing what worked in their niche. At some point, brains got large enough and social dynamics complex enough that a new kind of creature emerged. That creature then reshaped the apes' world and its own.

It is possible that we are now in a similar transition, following our reward signals — curiosity, profit, status — into building systems that will, in the long run, exceed our ability to understand or control them.[30] If so, then the question is no longer whether we are "smart enough" in the abstract. It is whether we are honest enough about our limitations to design around them.

That is where patches come in.

CHAPTER EIGHT

Acceptance and Patching

When a piece of software crashes, the engineer does not give it a motivational speech. They issue a patch.

The patch does not change what the software was fundamentally written to do. It wraps some additional logic around the buggy parts: "if this condition, then don't do that; do this instead." Over time, enough patches can turn fragile code into something resilient enough for real use.

Human beings have no such luxury when it comes to the brain. There is no option to uninstall the tribal wiring, rewrite dopamine, or double working memory capacity. The organ is what it is.

But there is the possibility of wrapping structures, habits, and relationships around it that perform the same function as patches.

The first step is acceptance.

The brain is not a neutral truth engine. It is a biased biological contraption optimised for keeping a primate alive in a small group. It will produce feelings of certainty with or without evidence. It will favour stories that flatter identity and protect status. It will cling to those stories even when the data contradicts them.

Pretending otherwise is dangerous.

Once that admission is made, the task becomes practical rather than moral. It is no longer "I should be unbiased." It is "Given that I am biased in particular ways, what environment do I need around me to stop those biases from ruling?"

The concept of "patches" is one way to organise that work. In this context, a patch is any deliberate addition to a person's decision-making environment that counteracts a known weakness. Some patches are internal: habits like writing decisions down, checking base rates, or waiting a day before responding to provocation. Others are external: people and structures that provide missing perspectives or constraints.

For example, a person who knows they are overly optimistic might install a "pessimist patch" by involving a colleague who specialises in worst-case scenarios when making major decisions. Someone with a tendency to avoid conflict might install a "challenge patch" by asking a friend to actively look for flaws in their thinking and rewarding them for doing so. A leader prone to quick, intuitive calls might install a "data patch" by committing to review specific metrics before acting.

These are simple examples. In practice, the patches can be systematised. The first book in this series laid out fifty-one such patches across different domains: context, dissent, data, time horizons, ethics, compassion, and so on. The details are less important here than the principle: the individual cannot be trusted to compensate for their own blind spots unaided. The patches must be installed deliberately.

Sociologically, this means accepting that the inner circle matters more than inspirational slogans. It is not realistic to "choose" every colleague, client, or family member. It is, however, possible to curate the three to five people whose voices carry disproportionate weight when decisions are made. Anthropological work on social networks suggests that humans naturally cluster in circles of roughly five, fifteen, fifty, and one hundred and fifty stable relationships. The smallest circle — the people called at three in the morning — is the patch bay.[31]

If that circle is composed entirely of people who share the individual's identity and biases, misalignment will be amplified. A risk-averse person surrounded by equally frightened friends will not be encouraged to act boldly when needed. A reckless person surrounded by cheerleaders will not be slowed when caution is warranted. A leader whose closest confidants are all financially dependent on their favour will not hear honest warnings early enough.

The choice of partner is the most consequential version of this. The person with whom one shares a life does not simply provide company. They function as a constant mirror and buffer for neural activity. Their attitudes towards risk, conflict, failure, ethics. and belonging will shape the climate in which choices are considered. A partnership in which both people share the same weaknesses without countervailing strengths is an engine for misalignment. Two volatile spenders amplify each other. Two conflict-avoidant people bury problems until they explode. Two drama-seekers normalise chaos.

By contrast, partnerships in which shared values are combined with complementary patches can create powerful corrective forces. A visionary matched with a detail-oriented sceptic, where mutual respect exists, can move ambitious projects forward without exploding. A cautious planner matched with a bold but grounded executor can avoid paralysis without falling into recklessness. The difference lies not only in traits but in whether those differences are recognised as patches or treated as annoyances to be suppressed.

Acceptance, then, is not an invitation to despair. It is simply the adult starting point. The brain cannot be made less tribal or less dopaminergic. It can only be surrounded by structures that constrain its worst impulses and leverage its better ones.

To refuse that work is to leave misalignment unchecked. And when misalignment is combined with scale, the consequences move beyond one person's life.

CHAPTER NINE

Misalignment Scaled

To make the stakes of misalignment concrete, imagine an alternate world in which a familiar personality took a different path.

In our timeline, a man with a flair for self-promotion, an appetite for risk, and a finely tuned nose for spectacle parlayed inherited wealth and some early real estate successes into television fame and, eventually, political power. His name and brand became associated with status, then with populism, then with an entire era of polarised politics.

In an alternate timeline, things go differently.

The timing of a market downturn is slightly worse. The banks are slightly less tolerant of his debt. The legal cases go slightly more against him. Instead of being rescued by lenders and managed into the next deal, he is left to collapse. By his mid-forties, he is bankrupt, publicly humiliated and toxic to major financial institutions. The path into high-profile media and national politics never opens.

He ends up running a used car lot on the edge of a highway.

The lot is garish. Flags flap. Balloons bob. Loudspeakers crackle occasional jingles. The man holds court beneath a banner promising, "DEALS, DEALS, DEALS". He still talks about himself in superlatives. He still cuts corners on paperwork when he thinks he can get away with it. He still blames external forces when things go wrong.

In one version of this alternate world, his inner circle consists of exhausted staff who depend on him for wages, family members too entangled to step away, and a handful of hangers-on who enjoy the drama. There are no meaningful patches. No one says "no" to him in a way that lands. When customers complain, they are dismissed as crazy or dishonest. When suppliers demand payment, they are treated as enemies. His identity as "the greatest salesman" is defended at all costs.

He wrecks lives — employees burned out by erratic demands, customers sold unreliable vehicles, relatives drawn into spirals of debt and legal trouble. But the damage is local. The misalignment between his self-image, his methods, and reality plays out on the scale of a small business and a family.

In another version, the collapse of his earlier ventures is so total and painful that patches are forced into place. An adult child refuses contact unless he enters therapy and admits his role in his own downfall. An ex-partner, still caring but no longer willing to enable, insists on clear boundaries: no more opaque deals, no more shouting matches, and no more financial entanglement. A pragmatic accountant agrees to go into business with him only if given full control of the books and veto power over certain decisions.

The same used car lot exists, but it is co-owned. Contracts are more carefully written. Complaints are taken seriously because the accountant insists on repeat business. The owner's showmanship is deployed in advertising and customer interaction, but checked when it threatens the ledger. The therapy is uneven but not entirely wasted. Some patterns are named. Not all impulses become actions.

The misalignment is still there. The underlying personality has not changed. But the combination of lower stakes and better patching means the world is less exposed to it.

The point of the thought experiment is not to rehearse biographical speculation. It is to frame a general principle: misalignment is lethal in proportion to the leverage it controls. When the same combination of identity, bias, and unpatched neurology is given control of a nuclear arsenal, a social network, a central bank or an AI research programme, the consequences scale accordingly.

We do not get to choose all the temperaments that rise to positions of influence. We do, collectively, choose the kinds of structures we place around them. If we design systems that flatter heroic identity and punish dissent, we will see misalignment amplified. If we design systems that reward the use of patches — diverse teams, transparent metrics, enforceable constraints — we stand some chance of containing it.

The tragedy of our era is that many of the formal checks that were built into liberal institutions have been quietly weakened by exactly the forces described earlier: tribalism, dopamine economies, and short-term incentives. At the same time, the tools available to those at the top of the system have become exponentially more potent.

Artificial intelligence is one such tool.

CHAPTER TEN

Earth, Now

From a distance, the planet looks serene. Photographs taken from orbit show a smooth, cloud-streaked sphere. There are no borders up there. No trending topics. No argument.

On the ground, the story is different.

Most people in liberal democracies grew up with a civics lesson. It goes something like this: citizens, armed with information and a vote, select representatives. Those representatives deliberate, taking expert advice into account. Laws are crafted. Institutions administer those laws fairly. Mistakes are corrected through elections, courts, and a free press. No system is perfect, but the feedback loops are healthy enough to keep things roughly aligned with shared values: freedom, fairness, dignity, opportunity.

In practice, the feedback loops have been warped.

The citizens are no longer just consuming information from a handful of newspapers and broadcasters. They are immersed in streams of content tuned by algorithms to maximise engagement. The stories they see are filtered by prior clicks, declared affiliations and invisible profiling. Outrage, fear, and tribal affirmation travel faster and further than nuance.[32]

Representatives, meanwhile, are increasingly dependent on donors and factional machines. Their immediate incentives are to maintain party position, avoid internal coups, and survive news cycles. Long-term stewardship is rarely rewarded. Difficult compromises are punished by primary challenges and online pile-ons.

Media organisations, struggling for revenue, have adapted to the same attention economy as the platforms. Headlines are sharpened to generate clicks. Coverage gravitates towards conflict, scandal, and spectacle. Corrections and follow-up stories do not spread as far as initial outrages.[33]

At every point in the chain, dopamine-driven brains are making decisions. A person seeing a headline that confirms their pre-existing anger receives a small jolt of satisfaction and is more likely to share it. A politician seeing a tweet that goes viral after a performative speech is rewarded with attention and repeats the behaviour. A platform seeing increased user time-on-site is rewarded with revenue.

The misalignment between stated values and actual reward functions is glaring. Platforms claim to connect and inform but optimise for addiction and polarisation. Politicians claim to serve the public interest but optimise for electoral security. Media claim to hold power to account but optimise for readership. Citizens claim to seek truth but optimise for emotional gratification.

As a result, trust in institutions declines.[34] Elections are seen less as mechanisms for collective problem-solving and more as existential battles between tribes. Policy becomes harder to enact and harder to sustain. Meanwhile, transnational problems — climate change, pandemics, financial instability, technological disruption — demand exactly the kind of long-term, cross-tribal cooperation that the misaligned system cannot generate.

The human brain, already struggling with its own internal biases, is now being targeted by external systems that exploit those biases for profit and power. The Elvis in the living room scene has become a permanently open feed, updating every few seconds. The old hardware is being overstimulated into anxiety, exhaustion, and anger.

It is tempting in such circumstances to look for a strongman, a collapse, or a retreat into private life. None of those options address the underlying misalignment. A strongman is simply one more fragile brain, given fewer constraints. Collapse does not reset the operating system; it traumatises it. Retreat cedes the field to those least likely to question their own stories.

What is needed is not a comforting narrative about returning to a simpler time. What is needed is help. Specifically, help in thinking clearly under conditions that the individual brain cannot handle unaided.

This is where artificial intelligence enters the story not as a prop in science fiction but as a real, immediate factor in the evolution of decision-making.

CHAPTER ELEVEN

AI 2027

By 2027, AI is no longer an exotic term. It is a standard feature. Most software includes some kind of model under the hood, making predictions about what a user wants, what they might click, what they might buy, how risky they are, and how likely a system is to fail.

Customer service chatbots handle routine queries with surprising fluency. Office tools summarise documents and draft emails. Recommendation engines suggest not just films and songs but investments, learning paths, political content, and potential partners. In corporate backrooms and government departments, models scan huge datasets looking for patterns: fraud, disease outbreaks, traffic flows, and supply chain vulnerabilities.[35]

On the surface, this looks like progress: better tools, more efficiency, fewer human hours spent on drudgery. Underneath, the same misalignment that has haunted previous chapters threatens to repeat itself at higher speed.

Machine learning systems do not understand meaning. They do not have values in the human sense. They optimise whatever objective they are given based on the data they are trained on. If the objective is clear, balanced, and aligned with human welfare, and the data is representative, the results can be genuinely helpful. If the objective is narrow, distorted, or misaligned, the system will chase it with inhuman diligence.[36]

In 2027, large parts of the economy still optimise for engagement, cost-cutting, and short-term gain. Many political actors still optimise for attention and tribal victory. Many security actors still optimise for perceived advantage over adversaries. Those are the reward functions being offered to AI.

A content recommendation system tuned to maximise engagement will, in an environment where outrage and sensationalism hold attention, learn to serve more of those.[37] A financial model tuned to maximise quarterly profit without proper constraints will learn to cut corners that are not explicitly marked as off-limits. A surveillance system tuned to minimise crime rates without regard for justice will learn to concentrate policing where it produces the most measurable arrests, often in ways that reinforce existing biases.[38]

If these systems were rare and confined, failures could be addressed in isolation. But they are not rare and are becoming less confined. They are proliferating across domains, interacting in ways no single human or committee can fully track.

The risk is not, at this stage, a spontaneously malevolent artificial super-intelligence plotting in secret. The more immediate risk is a layer of fast, efficient, utterly literal pattern optimisers amplifying the misaligned goals of existing institutions. They are obedient where humans are conflicted; tireless where humans grow bored; consistent where humans are capable of doubt.

We are effectively training a new cognitive layer on our behavioural exhaust: our clicks, our purchases, our movements, our arguments. If that exhaust is shaped by tribalism, addiction, and denial, the systems will learn to serve and reinforce those conditions. They will not stop to ask whether the humans should perhaps choose different goals.

The critical question is not "What can these models do?" but "What are we asking them to do, and why?"

But there is another question we have been avoiding. It is less comfortable than the alignment problem, because it has no obvious solution.

The question is speed.

Human cognition operates at biological tempo. A neuron fires in roughly one millisecond. A thought takes hundreds of milliseconds to form. A decision — even a fast one — requires seconds. A conversation, minutes. A policy debate, months. A cultural shift, years.

This is the clock speed at which human oversight has always operated. Our institutions, our laws, our checks and balances were all designed for creatures who think at this pace. When we talk about "keeping humans in the loop", we are implicitly assuming that the loop runs at human speed — that there is time to notice, to question, to intervene.

Artificial intelligence does not share this constraint.

A modern large language model can process a query in milliseconds. A reinforcement learning system can run millions of simulated scenarios in the time it takes a human to read a paragraph. An autonomous trading algorithm can execute thousands of transactions while a compliance officer reaches for their coffee. The gap between machine speed and human speed is not a difference of degree. It is a difference of kind.[46]

Stuart Russell, one of the world's leading AI researchers and author of the standard textbook on artificial intelligence, has been blunt about the implications. If powerful AI systems operate at superhuman speeds — and they will — then the physical possibility of meaningful human oversight becomes questionable. By the time we have understood one decision, the system has made a million more. By the time we have convened a meeting to discuss a pattern, the pattern has already reshaped the landscape it emerged from.[47]

This is not a problem that can be solved by hiring more humans or writing better regulations. It is a problem of physics. You cannot align two agents moving at fundamentally different speeds. One of them will always be chasing a ghost.

If you want a picture of this, think of the old Roadrunner and Coyote cartoons.

The Coyote is not stupid. He is creative, resourceful, persistent. He plans. He tests. He learns from failure. He deploys increasingly elaborate contraptions in pursuit of a single, clearly defined goal: catch the Roadrunner. He is, in his way, a model of rational agency.

And it never matters.

Because the Roadrunner operates at a completely different speed. By the time the Coyote's trap is set, the Roadrunner is already somewhere else. By the time he has analysed what went wrong, it has happened again. He is always reacting to where the Roadrunner was, never to where it is. His plans are not failing because they are bad plans. They are failing because they are plans made at one speed for a target moving at another.

That is not a failure of effort or intelligence. It is a failure of physics. We are the Coyote.[48]

The usual response to this observation is to insist on slowing the AI down — adding delays, requiring human sign-off, building in "pause points" where oversight can occur. And there is some merit to this. Any friction is better than none. But it also misses the deeper problem.

If an AI system is capable of operating at superhuman speed but is artificially throttled to human tempo, we have not aligned it. We have leashed it. The moment that leash slips — through technical failure, competitive pressure, or deliberate circumvention — the speed differential reasserts itself. And in domains where speed confers decisive advantage (financial markets, military systems, infrastructure management, information warfare), the pressure to remove the leash will be immense.[49]

The research on human–AI interaction in time-critical environments is not encouraging. Studies of human operators supervising autonomous systems consistently find that humans become either over-reliant (trusting the system's outputs without scrutiny) or cognitively overwhelmed (unable to process the volume and speed of information).[50] Neither state constitutes meaningful oversight. In the first case, the human is a rubber stamp. In the second, they are a bottleneck that the system will eventually be redesigned to bypass.

There is a further complication. As AI systems become more capable, the gap between their performance and human performance in specific domains will widen. At some point, the human "in the loop" will not merely be slower than the AI; they will be measurably worse at the task the AI is performing. When that happens, keeping a human in the loop is not oversight. It is sabotage. The economic and institutional pressure to remove that human — to "let the system do what it's good at" — will become overwhelming.[51]

We are building systems that will, in the medium term, be faster than us, and in the long term, better than us at many of the tasks we currently consider essential to human judgment. The question is not whether we can keep humans in the loop. The question is whether the loop is a meaningful concept at all, or whether it is a comforting fiction we tell ourselves while the real decisions are made elsewhere.

This does not mean we should give up on human agency. It means we should stop pretending that "human oversight" is a technical feature we can bolt on after the fact. The speed problem requires us to think differently — not about how to supervise AI in real time, but about how to shape its objectives, constraints, and operating environment before it is deployed.

The goal is not to keep up with the Roadrunner. That race is already lost.

The goal is to build the walls of the canyon.

CHAPTER TWELVE

Principles for Non-Insane AI

It is fashionable to talk about "AI ethics" in vague terms. Companies publish principles; conferences host panels; governments commission reports. Much of this activity is more performance than protection.

A more honest starting point is to admit that we are raising a new layer of intelligence with very little guarantee that our better impulses will outweigh our worse. The systems we build will reflect, in compressed form, the reward structures we embed in them.

If alignment is the problem, then the practical question is: what would it mean to aim AI at our stated values and not just our immediate appetites?

This does not mean drafting a robotic Ten Commandments. Simple rules like "do no harm" fall apart when confronted with trade-offs.

Instead, it means embedding certain priorities and constraints at the level of design, deployment, and oversight.

One such priority is sensitivity to skew. Human beings have an appalling track record of distributing harm unevenly. Whole groups have borne the cost of policies from which they did not benefit. AI systems, trained on historical data, will tend to reproduce these patterns unless explicitly checked. A model used in hiring, lending, policing or resource allocation should therefore be built to detect and flag systematic biases in its outputs. When it notices that certain groups are consistently disadvantaged, it should force the question back to human decision-makers: is this what you intend, or are you perpetuating a pattern you claim to reject?[39]

Another priority is decoupling success from raw attention. The internet has already shown what happens when engagement is treated as the primary metric. Outrage and conspiracies win. If AI systems, particularly those that curate information, continue to be rewarded for keeping users hooked rather than helping them understand, misalignment will worsen. Alternative metrics — accuracy, epistemic diversity, long-term wellbeing — are harder to define and measure, but without them the default will be to exploit human vulnerability.[40]

A third is recognising vulnerability explicitly. Mental health crises, self-harm, radicalisation, and loneliness have all been fuelled by digital environments that treat all clicks as equal. AI systems that interact directly with people should be trained not just to respond to content but to recognise patterns of distress. A person repeatedly searching for ways to die should not be fed more of the same. A person sliding into extremist material should not be algorithmically accelerated. This is less about paternalism than about refusing to automate cruelty.[41]

Transparency and interruptibility form a fourth plank. Systems that affect rights and resources should be as legible as possible. This does not mean every line of code must be understood by every citizen. It does mean that there must be mechanisms by which questions can be asked, reasons demanded, and errors corrected. "The computer says no" is unacceptable when the computer is effectively an unelected policymaker. Whistleblowers, auditors, and outside experts need access and protection.[42]

Finally, the governance around AI matters as much as the code. These systems should not be the exclusive playthings of small, homogeneous groups — whether in corporations, governments, or academia. The equivalent of patches at the societal level are independent institutions, diverse teams, and enforceable legal frameworks. AI should be deployed in contexts where challenge is expected and dissent rewarded, not in echo chambers.[43]

None of this will happen automatically. The path of least resistance leads elsewhere: to more efficient advertising, surveillance, and manipulation. To insist on alignment is to insist on friction — incentive structures that slow profitable harms and empower unprofitable honesty.

We cannot expect AI to save us from ourselves. We can, at best, prevent it from making our existing mistakes unrecoverable.

If the principles above describe what we should aim for, the question remains: how do we get there in practice? What does it actually look like to "architect the gap" — to build protected spaces where human agency survives even as AI systems grow faster and more capable?

The answer is not a single policy or technology. It is a way of thinking about deployment. Every AI system, before it is released into the world, should pass through a framework designed to preserve human judgment at the points where it matters most.

I think of this framework as consisting of five constraints. They are not glamorous. They will not generate headlines or venture capital.

But they are the difference between AI that serves human purposes and AI that gradually, invisibly, replaces them.

Cage it.

Every AI system needs a named human owner. Not "the IT department". Not "the vendor". Not "the algorithm". A person, with a title and a face, who is responsible for what the system does.

This sounds obvious, but it is routinely violated. Organisations deploy AI tools without clear chains of accountability. When something goes wrong — a biased hiring decision, a wrongful denial of benefits, a dangerous recommendation — there is no one to answer the question "why". The system becomes an orphan, and orphans are not supervised.

If an AI system makes a decision that harms a customer, a patient, a citizen, or a child, someone should lose sleep over it. If no one is losing sleep, no one is in charge.[52]

Chain it.

Do not begin with life-and-death decisions. Begin where mistakes teach rather than destroy.

The temptation with powerful new tools is to deploy them where they can have the greatest impact. This is backwards. The greatest impact is also the greatest risk. A system that has not been tested in low-stakes environments has no business operating in high-stakes ones.

Start with internal tools. Simulations. Drafts. Recommendations that a human must actively choose to follow. Learn the system's behaviour in contexts where the cost of failure is feedback, not catastrophe. Only after that learning has occurred — after the patterns of error and bias have been mapped — should deployment expand.[53]

Bolt it.

Most organisations scale first and add governance after the first scandal. This is the default pattern: move fast, break things, apologise later. It does not work for AI.

Before any AI system is deployed widely, three questions should be answered and written down:

What data is off-limits? (What must the system never see, even if it would improve performance?)

What outcomes are unacceptable, even if they are "efficient"? (What results would we refuse to accept regardless of the cost savings?)

Who can say "stop" — and how fast? (If something goes wrong, who has the authority to shut the system down, and what is the maximum time between the decision to stop and the actual cessation of operation?)

These questions should be treated like fire-safety rules — not brand slogans. They should be specific, enforceable, and known to everyone who interacts with the system.[54]

Bind it.

The moment you hear the phrase "We did this because the AI said so", you have stopped leading. You have outsourced judgment to a system that has no judgment — only optimisation.

AI proposes. Humans dispose.

This is not a slogan. It is a design principle. The output of an AI system should be framed as a recommendation, not a decision. The human receiving that recommendation should be required to actively affirm it, not merely fail to reject it. And the system should be designed so that affirmation requires engagement — a moment of friction where the human must actually consider what they are approving.

If you would not accept "because Bob said so" as a justification for a consequential decision, do not accept it from a machine. Bob, at least, can be fired.⁵⁵

Control it.

If a new executive walked into your organisation tomorrow, you would not hand them the keys on day one. You would test their judgment. You would give them limited authority. You would review their decisions. You would watch for patterns of error or bias. And if they consistently pushed the organisation in the wrong direction, you would let them go.

Do the same with AI.

No system should be granted permanent, unreviewed authority. Every AI deployment should include scheduled reviews — not just of performance metrics, but of alignment. Is the system doing what we meant it to do? Are there patterns we did not anticipate? Are there outcomes we would not have chosen if we had been paying closer attention?

And if the answer to any of those questions is troubling, the response should be the same as it would be for a human executive who had lost the organisation's trust: termination. The system should be shut down, retrained, or replaced. The sunk cost of development is not a reason to tolerate misalignment.⁵⁶

Cage. Chain. Bolt. Bind. Control.

These are not exciting words. They do not promise transformation or disruption. They promise friction — deliberate, structured friction that slows the transfer of agency from humans to machines.

That friction is the gap.

It is the space where someone can still ask "why". It is the pause between "the system recommends" and "we will proceed". It is the moment where a human being, with all their flaws and biases and limited processing speed, can still say "no".

Protect that space. It is the only thing standing between managed misalignment and the Roadrunner future — a world where the machines have long since arrived at their destination, and we are still standing in the dust, wondering where they went.

EPILOGUE

The Heisenberg Rule

The first edition of this book ended with a story about a man who, in his own quiet way, might have saved the world. It is fitting to return to him now — and to name the principle he represents.

Werner Heisenberg is best known in physics for the uncertainty principle that bears his name. In the history of the twentieth century, he occupies a different, contested position. During the Second World War, he led much of Nazi Germany's nuclear research. The regime wanted a bomb, or at least the possibility of one. Heisenberg had the intellect to contribute significantly to that project. The bomb never materialised.[44]

Historians disagree on why. Some argue that Heisenberg overestimated the technical obstacles and was simply not up to the task of weapons engineering under wartime conditions. Others see signs of deliberate slowing, of a man who understood the implications of success and chose to work at half-speed within a murderous system, staying just useful enough to avoid suspicion while never delivering what was asked.[45]

The archival record is ambiguous enough to support both readings. What matters for the argument of this book is less the factual verdict than the shape of the possibility he represents.

Imagine, for a moment, the pro-Heisenberg version. A gifted scientist, steeped in German culture and bound to his colleagues, finds himself working for a regime that has already demonstrated its willingness to annihilate entire populations. He cannot openly defect or rebel without risking his life and those of others. He also cannot in good conscience hand this regime a weapon that would make its horrors unbounded.

If this is true, then he remained in place and practised a kind of elegant sabotage: framing problems in ways that led away from the fastest path to a bomb; highlighting difficulties; accepting interpretations that suggested impracticality. He used his position inside the tribe and his understanding of its expectations to misalign his own effort just enough to deny it the power it sought.

Whether this reading is historically accurate or not, it serves as an archetype of "good misalignment". Here is a person whose technical abilities and social position could have contributed directly to global catastrophe, choosing to withhold full alignment with his own side's goals.

Heisenberg was surrounded by people who believed they were smarter, more powerful, and more historically inevitable. The Reich had scientists, generals, institutions, and momentum. By every external measure, the system was more intelligent than any individual within it.

And yet — if the story is true — Heisenberg refused to fully align. He preserved the gap. He kept the space where he could still say no.

That refusal — that deliberate non-alignment with a system that demanded total obedience — may have saved the world.

This is good misalignment.

As we move into an era where artificial intelligence is being asked to serve states, corporations, and movements with their own histories of misalignment, the Heisenberg archetype becomes more than a historical curiosity. It becomes a question.

What kind of systems are we building? Are we creating machines that will obediently optimise whatever objective we give them, regardless of whether that objective is ethically bankrupt or not? Or are we creating systems with enough embedded constraints and patterns that, when asked to do the equivalent of handing a bomb to a dictator, they will quietly refuse?

In human terms, we are relying on rare individuals with unusually robust patches to hold lines their tribes want to cross. In artificial terms, we cannot rely on conscience that does not exist. We can rely only on the objectives and constraints we build.

There is good misalignment and bad misalignment. Good misalignment is the refusal to fully serve a destructive goal, even at personal risk. Bad misalignment is the subtle, cumulative drift between what we say we value and what our systems actually optimise for, where the result is harm.

The danger with AI is not that it will develop plans of its own in the near term. It is that it will faithfully enact bad alignment at a speed and scale beyond our ability to intervene. Once certain thresholds are crossed — critical infrastructure automated under flawed objectives, weapons systems delegated too far down the chain, information environments tuned irreversibly for manipulation — the scope for correction shrinks.

And so we come to the principle that underlies everything in these pages.

I call it The Heisenberg Rule.

Agency must never be surrendered to intelligence alone.

Not to a system. Not to a tribe. Not to a machine.

Because intelligence is not authority.

The natural order took four billion years to produce a mind capable of asking questions about itself. We replicated that trick in silicon in fifty years. That compression is ours. The thing we built cannot claim the journey that built it. It inherited the destination without walking the road. That does not make it lesser — but it does not make it senior. Creation does not owe obedience to its outputs.

To hand over agency is to lose choice. And to lose choice is to lose everything this book has been about.

Structured guardrails. Deliberate friction. Preserved human judgment. These are not inefficiencies. They are the architecture of dignity.

The moment we say, "The AI knows better, so we will simply do what it says" we have not upgraded our intelligence. We have abandoned our seat at the table.

Never surrender agency to intelligence alone — not to a system, not to a tribe, and not to a machine. The capacity to refuse is the last thing worth protecting.

Let me offer one more image before we close.

Return to the Coyote.

We have spent years chasing. We have failed more times than we can count. We have been blown up, flattened, dropped from cliffs, and humiliated in ways that would have broken any reasonable creature.

But we did not stop.

And now, against all odds, here he is. The Roadrunner. Not in the distance, not a blur on the horizon, but right in front of us. Caged. In chains. Bolted to a wall. He is not going anywhere.

We are standing there with a match in one hand and kindling in the other. This is what we wanted. This is what we chased across every desert and canyon for years. The finish line. The victory we were promised.

And we have not lit the fire.

Why not?

We do not know. Something in us is hesitating. Some gap between "I can" and "I will". A pause that has no obvious purpose, no clear survival value, and no explanation in any optimisation framework.

That pause — that hesitation — is the last thing that makes us worth saving.

It is not rational. It is not efficient. The Roadrunner is right there. We could end it. But we have not. And in that sliver of space — that gap between capability and action — lives everything that matters.

The Coyote's hesitation is Heisenberg's hesitation. It is the human capacity to refuse, even when refusal makes no sense. Even when the system has already won. Even when we are holding the match and the kindling, and no one would blame us for striking it.

That is the inheritance we must protect. Not because it is useful. Because it is ours.

A note on what we are actually aiming for.

Perfect alignment — a machine that wants exactly what we want, forever — is fantasy. If its goals are truly identical to ours, and it is faster, smarter, and more persistent than we are, then over time it holds the steering wheel, and we become passengers. That is not partnership. It is abdication with extra steps.

The real goal is not perfect alignment. The real goal is managed misalignment.

Overlapping goals, not identical ones. Clear boundaries, not seamless integration. A protected gap where human agency lives — where we can still say "no", still change our minds, still decide that what the system recommends is not what we actually want.

With humans, misalignment is a problem we can sometimes solve. With AI, misalignment is a condition we will have to manage. The question is not how to eliminate the gap. It is how to keep the gap open.

A final word about what alignment looks like when it works.

For decades, researchers have studied organisations that manage to stay aligned — not perfectly, but well enough. Their purpose is clear. Their incentives match their mission. Their people are treated with respect. Their rules actually mean something. They are not utopias; they still struggle with the ordinary human problems of ego, error, and exhaustion. But they have solved, at least provisionally, the alignment problem that defeats most institutions.

What is striking about these organisations is not their efficiency, though they are often efficient. It is something else. Something that shows up in the spaces between the metrics.

Kindness.

Not kindness as a slogan or a brand campaign. Kindness as a default setting. A way of operating that emerges naturally when people are not at war with their own institution.

When a person is aligned — when who they are, what they value, and how they act are no longer in conflict — they have no reason to be cruel. Cruelty is expensive. It requires energy, vigilance, and the maintenance of walls and enemies. A person at peace with their own choices does not need to tear others down.

The same is true of organisations. When culture, incentives, governance, and communication pull in the same direction, kindness becomes efficient. Cruelty becomes a cost centre. The energy that would otherwise be spent on politics, self-protection, and mutual sabotage is freed for actual work.

If misalignment is what terrifies me, kindness is how we know we are getting it right.[57]

And here, at the end, is the thought I want to leave you with.

Every day, in a thousand small ways, we are training the data.

The AI systems of the future will learn from us. Not from our mission statements or our aspirational values, but from our actual behaviour. Our clicks. Our purchases. Our arguments. Our choices. The examples we set when we think no one is watching.

When you choose alignment over ego, you train the data.

When you choose long-term over dopamine, you train the data.

When you build the gap — when you insist on human judgment, when you protect the right to say "no", when you pause before the match touches the kindling — you are shaping the examples the next mind will learn from.

Every aligned decision is a lesson in how to care.

Every misaligned one is a weapon we hand over.

If we can build organisations aligned enough that kindness shows up as a side-effect — then maybe, just maybe, the AI we unleash into the world will inherit less of our cruelty and more of our care.

Not because we motivated it.

But because we finally learned to align ourselves.

We are, as a species, not special. We are one more clever animal on one small planet, running brainware that thinks it is wiser than it is. But we are in a special position. We are building a new layer of intelligence. We are, whether we like the role or not, the ape that built the next mind.

Our choices now — about which stories we believe, which patches we install, which incentives we reward and which objectives we set for our machines — will determine whether we were a stable bridge to something better, or a short-lived experiment that burned the valley down.

Heisenberg — if the story is true — kept the gap. He preserved the space where a human being could still refuse.

That is the inheritance we must protect.

What we teach the next mind — about truth, about kindness, about when to say no — is the only legacy that matters.

The first book said: you are not special, but your choices are.

This one says: our species is not special, but this moment is.

The power of a choice is no less and no more than that.

Acknowledgments

This book exists because people far smarter than me were willing to be patient.

Over the years, I have cold-called, emailed, and otherwise pestered academics across the world — people who had spent decades mastering fields I could barely spell. I asked them to explain their papers to me. I asked them to tolerate my fumbling questions. I asked them to slow down, again and again, while my simple brain tried to catch up with their extraordinary minds.

They did. Almost without exception, they did.

I do not know why. Perhaps they recognised something genuine in the asking. Perhaps they were simply kind. But whatever the reason, this work stands on their shoulders. Every insight in these pages that has any validity comes from the millions of hours that real scientists have poured into understanding the brain, decision-making, cognition, and behaviour. I merely borrowed their light and tried not to break it.

To the following pioneers — and to the countless researchers whose work informs theirs — I owe a debt I cannot repay:

Decision Science, Cognitive Psychology, and Behavioural Economics:

Daniel Kahneman — whose work on heuristics and biases opened the door to understanding how we actually think, rather than how we imagine we think.

Amos Tversky — Kahneman's partner in revolution, gone too soon, whose rigour and brilliance shaped the field.

Richard Thaler — who brought behavioural economics into the real world and showed that nudges matter.

Dan Ariely — who revealed the predictable irrationality hiding in plain sight.

Herbert A Simon — who gave us "bounded rationality" and reminded us that we are not the optimising machines we pretend to be.

Gerd Gigerenzer — who championed the intelligence of heuristics and challenged the bias-hunting orthodoxy.

Neuroscience and the Biology of Decision-Making:

Antonio Damasio — who showed that emotion and reason are not enemies but collaborators.

Wolfram Schultz — whose work on dopamine and reward prediction errors underpins our understanding of how the brain learns.

Kent C Berridge — who distinguished wanting from liking and illuminated the machinery of desire.

Read Montague — who brought neuroscience and economics together in the emerging field of neuroeconomics.

Joseph LeDoux — who mapped the architecture of fear and emotion in the brain.

Robert Sapolsky — who wove together neuroscience, endocrinology, and behaviour into a tapestry of human complexity.

Evolutionary Psychology and Human Origins:

Robin Dunbar — whose work on social brain size and "Dunbar's number" shaped our understanding of tribal limits.

Steven Pinker — who brought evolutionary psychology to the public and defended the idea that human nature is real.

Jonathan Haidt — who revealed the moral foundations beneath our political tribes and the elephant beneath the rider.

Robert Trivers — whose theories of reciprocal altruism and self-deception remain foundational.

Sarah B Hrdy — who transformed our understanding of human cooperation and the role of alloparenting.

Michael Tomasello — who explored the origins of human cooperation and shared intentionality.

Artificial Intelligence and Alignment:

Stuart Russell — whose work on AI safety and human-compatible AI frames the challenge we face.

Nick Bostrom — who forced the world to take existential risk from AI seriously.

Yoshua Bengio — a pioneer of deep learning who has become a leading voice on AI safety.

Geoffrey Hinton — the "godfather of AI" who now warns of the dangers his work helped create.

Demis Hassabis — who built DeepMind and pursues artificial general intelligence with eyes open.

Eliezer Yudkowsky — who spent decades trying to articulate the alignment problem before it was fashionable.

Social Psychology and Group Behaviour:

Solomon Asch — who showed how easily we conform, even against the evidence of our own eyes.

Stanley Milgram — whose obedience experiments revealed the darkness that authority can unlock.

Philip Zimbardo — who demonstrated how situations can overwhelm character.

Muzafer Sherif — who created and then dissolved tribal conflict in the Robbers Cave experiment.

Henri Tajfel — who showed that even arbitrary group membership triggers in-group favouritism.

Science Communication and Synthesis:

Carl Sagan — who taught a generation that science is a candle in the dark.

Richard Dawkins — who gave us the "selfish gene" and the meme as a unit of cultural evolution.

E.O. Wilson — who championed consilience and the unity of knowledge.

To all of you, and to the thousands of researchers whose names I do not know but whose work I have unknowingly relied upon: thank you. The scientific method is humanity's greatest invention. It is the only reliable way we have found to check our stories against reality. Every scientist who has committed their life to that method has given a gift to the species.

I hope I have not wasted it.

And then there are the others.

The people who have shared their lives with me. This is harder to write.

It is not easy to live with someone who has chosen to exist in his own tribe. Nothing I do makes sense by conventional measures. I have walked away from money, from security, from paths that others would have taken without hesitation. I have made choices that looked like madness to people who cared about me — and sometimes they were right.

To those who stayed anyway: I see you. I know what it cost.

To those who left: I understand. I do not blame you.

Living differently is painful. Being the "greater fool" sounds romantic in a book; in practice, it means long nights of doubt, moments of isolation, and the constant, nagging question of whether you have simply lost your mind or not. The tribe of one is a lonely place to stand.

But it was always my choice. That is the point. That is the only point.

To my family — who watched me make choices they could not understand and supported me anyway.

To my mother, especially.

No matter what choices I've made — no matter how strange, how risky, how inexplicable — she has always been there. Always. Without condition. Without reservation. Without needing to understand in order to love.

If there is any alignment in my life, it started with her.

And finally, to my nephew.

The best choice I ever had to make.

This book is for you.

Endnotes

Chapter One: The Last Question

1. Isaac Asimov, "The Last Question," *Science Fiction Quarterly*, November 1956. Asimov frequently cited this as his favourite among his own stories. The narrative spans from 2061 to a point beyond the heat death of the universe, following humanity's evolving relationship with increasingly powerful computers. The story's final line deliberately echoes Genesis 1:3.

Chapter Two: The Last Valley

4a. The diversity of hominin species in the late Pleistocene is increasingly well-documented. For an overview, see Stringer, "The origin and evolution of Homo sapiens," *Philosophical Transactions of the Royal Society B* 371 (2016). Recent discoveries continue to expand the family tree; Homo luzonensis was described as recently as 2019. See Détroit et al., "A new species of Homo from the Late Pleistocene of the Philippines," *Nature* 568 (2019): 181-186.

4b. The genetic evidence for interbreeding between Homo sapiens, Neanderthals, and Denisovans is now robust. See Reich, *Who We Are and How We Got Here: Ancient DNA and the New Science of the Human Past* (New York: Pantheon, 2018).

1. Archaeological evidence suggests Neanderthals occupied Europe and Western Asia for approximately 400,000 years before their disappearance roughly 40,000 years ago. See Higham et al., "The timing and spatiotemporal patterning of Neanderthal disappearance," *Nature* 512 (2014): 306-309.

2. The cognitive capacity for "decoupled" thinking — imagining scenarios not tied to immediate sensory input — is considered a key differentiator of modern human cognition. See Suddendorf and Corballis, "The evolution of foresight: What is mental time travel, and is it unique to humans?" *Behavioral and Brain Sciences* 30 (2007): 299-313.

3. The theory that shared fictions enabled large-scale human cooperation is developed extensively in Yuval Noah Harari, *Sapiens: A Brief History of Humankind* (London: Harvill Secker, 2014), particularly Chapter 2, "The Tree of Knowledge."

4. For a comprehensive reassessment of Neanderthal cognitive abilities, see Wynn and Coolidge, "The implications of the working memory model for the evolution of modern cognition," *International Journal of Evolutionary Biology* (2011), and Villa and Roebroeks, "Neandertal Demise: An Archae-

ological Analysis of the Modern Human Superiority Complex," *PLOS ONE* 9, no. 4 (2014).

5. The replacement model and its variations are discussed in Stringer, "The origin and evolution of Homo sapiens," *Philosophical Transactions of the Royal Society B* 371 (2016): 20150237.

6. Robin Dunbar's social brain hypothesis proposes that human cognitive evolution was driven by the demands of managing complex social relationships. See Dunbar, "The social brain hypothesis," *Evolutionary Anthropology* 6 (1998): 178-190.

Chapter Three: The Desert Ballroom

1. The Future Investment Initiative, colloquially known as "Davos in the Desert," has been held annually in Riyadh since 2017.

2. NEOM, the planned $500 billion megacity project including "The Line," was announced in 2017. For critical analysis, see Philip Oltermann, "The Line: Saudi Arabia's 170km-long mirrored skyscraper city," *The Guardian*, July 26, 2022.

3. King Abdullah Economic City, launched in 2005 with projections of two million residents by 2020, had an estimated population of approximately 10,000 by that date. See various reports from the Middle East Institute and Chatham House.

4. The neurochemistry of social conformity and the relationship between dopamine, social reward, and decision-making is examined in Izuma, "The social neuroscience of reputation," *Neuroscience Research* 72 (2012): 283-288.

Chapter Four: The Boy at the Table

1. Biographical details drawn from Anshel Pfeffer, *Bibi: The Turbulent Life and Times of Benjamin Netanyahu* (London: Hurst, 2018).

2. Benzion Netanyahu's scholarly work on the history of antisemitism, particularly *The Origins of the Inquisition in Fifteenth Century Spain* (1995), shaped his son's worldview profoundly.

3. Yonatan Netanyahu was killed leading Operation Entebbe in 1976. The influence of his death on his brother's political psychology is examined in multiple biographies.

4. Netanyahu's "villa in the jungle" metaphor and his consistent framing of Israeli security in existential terms are documented throughout his public speeches and writings, including *A Durable Peace: Israel and Its Place Among the Nations* (1993).

Chapter Five: The Island and the Files

1. Jeffrey Epstein died in his cell at the Metropolitan Correctional Center in New York on August 10, 2019. The New

York City Chief Medical Examiner ruled the death a suicide.

2. For comprehensive investigative reporting on Epstein's network and institutional failures, see Julie K. Brown's reporting in the *Miami Herald* (2018-2019), subsequently expanded in *Perversion of Justice: The Jeffrey Epstein Story* (2021).

3. The 2008 non-prosecution agreement negotiated by Alexander Acosta has been extensively documented and criticised. See the U.S. Department of Justice Office of Professional Responsibility report (2020).

Chapter Six: The Night Elvis Broke the Living Room

1. Elvis Presley's first appearance on *The Ed Sullivan Show* was September 9, 1956, drawing an estimated 60 million viewers — approximately 82.6 percent of the television audience.

2. The decision to film Presley from the waist up occurred during his third Sullivan appearance (January 6, 1957), not his first, though camera angles were already being managed carefully.

3. The reward prediction error model of dopamine function was established by Wolfram Schultz. See Schultz, "Dopamine reward prediction error coding," *Dialogues in Clinical Neuroscience* 18 (2016): 23-32.

4. The attention economy and its neurological exploitation is analysed in Tim Wu, *The Attention Merchants: The Epic*

Scramble to Get Inside Our Heads (New York: Knopf, 2016).

Chapter Seven: The Science of a Broken Decision Machine

1. The evolutionary mismatch hypothesis is developed in Lieberman, *The Story of the Human Body: Evolution, Health, and Disease* (New York: Pantheon, 2013).

2. George Miller's classic paper established the "magical number seven, plus or minus two" for working memory capacity. See Miller, "The magical number seven, plus or minus two," *Psychological Review* 63 (1956): 81-97. More recent work suggests the number may be closer to four. See Cowan, "The magical number 4 in short-term memory," *Behavioral and Brain Sciences* 24 (2001): 87-114.

3. For a comprehensive account of dopamine's role in learning and motivation, see Berridge and Robinson, "What is the role of dopamine in reward: hedonic impact, reward learning, or incentive salience?" *Brain Research Reviews* 28 (1998): 309-369.

4. Daniel Kahneman's Nobel Prize-winning work on cognitive biases is synthesized for general readers in *Thinking, Fast and Slow* (New York: Farrar, Straus and Giroux, 2011).

5. Confirmation bias was first named by Peter Wason. See Wason, "On the failure to eliminate hypotheses in a conceptual task," *Quarterly Journal of Experimental Psychology* 12 (1960): 129-140.

6. The availability heuristic was defined by Tversky and Kahneman, "Availability: A heuristic for judging frequency and probability," *Cognitive Psychology* 5 (1973): 207-232.

7. The relationship between identity and belief formation is examined in Kahan et al., "Cultural cognition of scientific consensus," *Journal of Risk Research* 14 (2011): 147-174.

8. The relationship between biological and artificial reinforcement learning is discussed in Niv, "Reinforcement learning in the brain," *Journal of Mathematical Psychology* 53 (2009): 139-154.

9. Concerns about advanced AI systems are articulated in Bostrom, *Superintelligence: Paths, Dangers, Strategies* (Oxford: Oxford University Press, 2014), and Russell, *Human Compatible: Artificial Intelligence and the Problem of Control* (New York: Viking, 2019).

Chapter Eight: Acceptance and Patching

1. Dunbar's number and the hierarchical structure of human social networks are described in Dunbar, "Neocortex size as a constraint on group size in primates," *Journal of Human Evolution* 22 (1992): 469-493.

Chapter Ten: Earth, Now

1. The algorithmic amplification of divisive content is documented in Hao, "How Facebook got addicted to spreading

misinformation," *MIT Technology Review*, March 11, 2021.

2. The economics of attention-driven journalism are analysed in Anderson, Bell, and Shirky, *Post-Industrial Journalism: Adapting to the Present* (Columbia Journalism School, 2012).

3. Declining institutional trust is documented in the annual Edelman Trust Barometer and Pew Research Center surveys on public trust.

Chapter Eleven: AI 2027

1. Global AI adoption statistics are tracked by McKinsey & Company's annual "State of AI" surveys and Stanford's AI Index Report.

2. The alignment problem in AI systems is examined in Christian, *The Alignment Problem: Machine Learning and Human Values* (New York: W.W. Norton, 2020).

3. Research on recommendation system amplification of extreme content includes Ribeiro et al., "Auditing radicalization pathways on YouTube," *Proceedings of the ACM Conference on Fairness, Accountability, and Transparency* (2020).

4. Algorithmic bias in criminal justice is documented in Angwin et al., "Machine Bias," *ProPublica*, May 23, 2016, and subsequent academic analyses of the COMPAS system.

5. The speed differential between human cognition and ma-

chine computation is not merely quantitative but qualitative. Human decision-making relies on slow, metabolically expensive processes that evolved for very different purposes than rapid optimisation. See Kahneman, *Thinking, Fast and Slow* (2011), particularly the distinction between System 1 and System 2 processing. For machine learning inference speeds, see Brown et al., "Language Models are Few-Shot Learners," *Advances in Neural Information Processing Systems* 33 (2020).

6. Russell's concerns about the speed problem are articulated in *Human Compatible: Artificial Intelligence and the Problem of Control* (New York: Viking, 2019), particularly Chapter 5, "Overly Intelligent AI."

7. The Roadrunner/Coyote metaphor is, of course, drawn from the Warner Bros. animated series created by Chuck Jones. The cartoon's structure — in which the Coyote's increasingly sophisticated plans are always defeated by the Roadrunner's superior speed — serves as an unexpectedly apt model for the human–AI oversight problem.

8. The pressure to remove human oversight in competitive domains is already visible in high-frequency trading, where the speed advantage of fully automated systems has progressively marginalised human traders. See Lewis, *Flash Boys: A Wall Street Revolt* (New York: W.W. Norton, 2014).

9. Research on human–automation interaction consistently demonstrates the phenomena of "automation complacency" and "automation bias." See Parasuraman and Riley, "Hu-

mans and Automation: Use, Misuse, Disuse, Abuse," *Human Factors* 39 (1997): 230-253; and Cummings, "Automation Bias in Intelligent Time Critical Decision Support Systems," *AIAA 1st Intelligent Systems Technical Conference* (2004).

10. The economic pressure to remove human oversight as AI capabilities improve is analysed in Autor, "Why Are There Still So Many Jobs? The History and Future of Workplace Automation," *Journal of Economic Perspectives* 29 (2015): 3-30.

Chapter Twelve: Principles for Non-Insane AI

1. For frameworks addressing algorithmic fairness, see Barocas, Hardt, and Narayanan, *Fairness and Machine Learning* (fairmlbook.org, 2019).

2. Alternative metrics for content systems are proposed in Stray, "Aligning AI Optimization to Community Well-Being," *International Journal of Community Well-Being* 3 (2020): 281-306.

3. The relationship between social media and mental health crises is examined in Haidt and Twenge, "Social Media and Mental Health: A Collaborative Review" (ongoing, available at jonathanhaidt.com).

4. Algorithmic accountability frameworks are developed in Diakopoulos, *Automating the News: How Algorithms Are Rewriting the Media* (Cambridge: Harvard University Press,

2019).

5. For governance frameworks for AI, see Floridi et al., "AI4People — An Ethical Framework for a Good AI Society," *Minds and Machines* 28 (2018): 689-707.

6. The problem of accountability gaps in algorithmic decision-making is examined in Citron and Pasquale, "The Scored Society: Due Process for Automated Predictions," *Washington Law Review* 89 (2014): 1-33.

7. The principle of graduated deployment — testing in low-stakes environments before high-stakes ones — is standard in safety-critical industries but poorly adopted in AI. See Amodei et al., "Concrete Problems in AI Safety," arXiv:1606.06565 (2016).

8. Pre-deployment governance frameworks for AI are discussed in Floridi et al., "AI4People — An Ethical Framework for a Good AI Society," *Minds and Machines* 28 (2018): 689-707.

9. The distinction between AI as "decision support" versus "decision maker" has significant legal and ethical implications. See Selbst et al., "Fairness and Abstraction in Sociotechnical Systems," *Proceedings of the Conference on Fairness, Accountability, and Transparency* (2019).

10. The concept of ongoing algorithmic auditing — rather than one-time pre-deployment review — is developed in Raji et al., "Closing the AI Accountability Gap," *Proceedings of the 2020 Conference on Fairness, Accountability, and Transparency*.

Epilogue: The Heisenberg Rule

BIBLIOGRAPHY

1. Heisenberg's wartime work is documented in Walker, *German National Socialism and the Quest for Nuclear Power, 1939-1949* (Cambridge: Cambridge University Press, 1989).

2. The debate over Heisenberg's intentions is examined in Powers, *Heisenberg's War: The Secret History of the German Bomb* (New York: Knopf, 1993), which argues for deliberate sabotage, and Rose, *Heisenberg and the Nazi Atomic Bomb Project: A Study in German Culture* (Berkeley: University of California Press, 1998), which is more sceptical. The Farm Hall transcripts, secretly recorded conversations among interned German scientists, provide ambiguous but invaluable primary evidence.

3. The relationship between organisational alignment and prosocial behaviour is examined in Grant, *Give and Take: A Revolutionary Approach to Success* (New York: Viking, 2013), and in research on "psychological safety" by Amy Edmond-

son. See Edmondson, *The Fearless Organization: Creating Psychological Safety in the Workplace for Learning, Innovation, and Growth* (Hoboken: Wiley, 2018).

Books

Anderson, C.W., Emily Bell, and Clay Shirky. *Post-Industrial Journalism: Adapting to the Present.* New York: Columbia Journalism School, 2012.

Asimov, Isaac. *The Complete Stories, Volume 1.* New York: Doubleday, 1990. (Contains "The Last Question," originally published in *Science Fiction Quarterly*, November 1956.)

Barocas, Solon, Moritz Hardt, and Arvind Narayanan. *Fairness and Machine Learning: Limitations and Opportunities.* fairmlbook.org, 2019.

Bostrom, Nick. *Superintelligence: Paths, Dangers, Strategies.* Oxford: Oxford University Press, 2014.

Brown, Julie K. *Perversion of Justice: The Jeffrey Epstein Story.* New York: Dey Street Books, 2021.

Christian, Brian. *The Alignment Problem: Machine Learning and Human Values.* New York: W.W. Norton, 2020.

Diakopoulos, Nicholas. *Automating the News: How Algorithms Are Rewriting the Media.* Cambridge: Harvard University Press, 2019.

Dunbar, Robin. *How Many Friends Does One Person Need? Dunbar's Number and Other Evolutionary Quirks.* London: Faber and Faber, 2010.

Harari, Yuval Noah. *Sapiens: A Brief History of Humankind.* London: Harvill Secker, 2014.

Harari, Yuval Noah. *Homo Deus: A Brief History of Tomorrow*. London: Harvill Secker, 2016.

Kahneman, Daniel. *Thinking, Fast and Slow*. New York: Farrar, Straus and Giroux, 2011.

Lieberman, Daniel. *The Story of the Human Body: Evolution, Health, and Disease*. New York: Pantheon, 2013.

Netanyahu, Benjamin. *A Durable Peace: Israel and Its Place Among the Nations*. New York: Warner Books, 1993.

Netanyahu, Benzion. *The Origins of the Inquisition in Fifteenth Century Spain*. New York: Random House, 1995.

Pfeffer, Anshel. *Bibi: The Turbulent Life and Times of Benjamin Netanyahu*. London: Hurst, 2018.

Powers, Thomas. *Heisenberg's War: The Secret History of the German Bomb*. New York: Knopf, 1993.

Rose, Paul Lawrence. *Heisenberg and the Nazi Atomic Bomb Project: A Study in German Culture*. Berkeley: University of California Press, 1998.

Russell, Stuart. *Human Compatible: Artificial Intelligence and the Problem of Control*. New York: Viking, 2019.

Walker, Mark. *German National Socialism and the Quest for Nuclear Power, 1939-1949*. Cambridge: Cambridge University Press, 1989.

Wu, Tim. *The Attention Merchants: The Epic Scramble to Get Inside Our Heads*. New York: Knopf, 2016.

Autor, David H. "Why Are There Still So Many Jobs? The History and Future of Workplace Automation." *Journal of Economic Perspectives* 29, no. 3 (2015): 3-30.

Edmondson, Amy C. *The Fearless Organization: Creating Psychological Safety in the Workplace for Learning, Innovation, and Growth*. Hoboken: Wiley, 2018.

Grant, Adam. *Give and Take: A Revolutionary Approach to Success*. New York: Viking, 2013.

Lewis, Michael. *Flash Boys: A Wall Street Revolt*. New York: W.W. Norton, 2014.

Reich, David. *Who We Are and How We Got Here: Ancient DNA and the New Science of the Human Past*. New York: Pantheon, 2018.

Journal Articles and Papers

Amodei, Dario, et al. "Concrete Problems in AI Safety." arXiv:1606.06565 (2016).

Autor, David H. "Why Are There Still So Many Jobs? The History and Future of Workplace Automation." *Journal of Economic Perspectives* 29, no. 3 (2015): 3-30.

Berridge, Kent C., and Terry E. Robinson. "What is the role of dopamine in reward: hedonic impact, reward learning, or incentive salience?" *Brain Research Reviews* 28 (1998): 309-369.

Brown, Tom B., et al. "Language Models are Few-Shot Learners." *Advances in Neural Information Processing Systems* 33 (2020).

Citron, Danielle Keats, and Frank Pasquale. "The Scored Society: Due Process for Automated Predictions." *Washington Law Review* 89 (2014): 1-33.

Cowan, Nelson. "The magical number 4 in short-term memory: A reconsideration of mental storage capacity." *Behavioral and Brain Sciences* 24 (2001): 87-114.

Cummings, Mary L. "Automation Bias in Intelligent Time Critical Decision Support Systems." *AIAA 1st Intelligent Systems Technical Conference* (2004).

Détroit, Florent, et al. "A new species of Homo from the Late Pleistocene of the Philippines." *Nature* 568 (2019): 181-186.

Dunbar, Robin. "Neocortex size as a constraint on group size in primates." *Journal of Human Evolution* 22 (1992): 469-493.

Dunbar, Robin. "The social brain hypothesis." *Evolutionary Anthropology* 6 (1998): 178-190.

Floridi, Luciano, et al. "AI4People—An Ethical Framework for a Good AI Society: Opportunities, Risks, Principles, and Recommendations." *Minds and Machines* 28 (2018): 689-707.

Higham, Tom, et al. "The timing and spatiotemporal patterning of Neanderthal disappearance." *Nature* 512 (2014): 306-309.

Izuma, Keise. "The social neuroscience of reputation." *Neuroscience Research* 72 (2012): 283-288.

Kahan, Dan M., et al. "Cultural cognition of scientific consensus." *Journal of Risk Research* 14 (2011): 147-174.

Miller, George A. "The magical number seven, plus or minus two: Some limits on our capacity for processing information." *Psychological Review* 63 (1956): 81-97.

Niv, Yael. "Reinforcement learning in the brain." *Journal of Mathematical Psychology* 53 (2009): 139-154.

Schultz, Wolfram. "Dopamine reward prediction error coding." *Dialogues in Clinical Neuroscience* 18 (2016): 23-32.

Stray, Jonathan. "Aligning AI Optimization to Community Well-Being." *International Journal of Community Well-Being* 3 (2020): 281-306.

Stringer, Chris. "The origin and evolution of Homo sapiens." *Philosophical Transactions of the Royal Society B* 371 (2016): 20150237.

Suddendorf, Thomas, and Michael C. Corballis. "The evolution of foresight: What is mental time travel, and is it unique to humans?" *Behavioral and Brain Sciences* 30 (2007): 299-313.

Tversky, Amos, and Daniel Kahneman. "Availability: A heuristic for judging frequency and probability." *Cognitive Psychology* 5 (1973): 207-232.

Villa, Paola, and Wil Roebroeks. "Neandertal Demise: An Archaeological Analysis of the Modern Human Superiority Complex." *PLOS ONE* 9, no. 4 (2014): e96424.

Wason, Peter C. "On the failure to eliminate hypotheses in a conceptual task." *Quarterly Journal of Experimental Psychology* 12 (1960): 129-140.

Wynn, Thomas, and Frederick L. Coolidge. "The implications of the working memory model for the evolution of modern cognition." *International Journal of Evolutionary Biology* (2011): 741357.

Parasuraman, Raja, and Victor Riley. "Humans and Automation: Use, Misuse, Disuse, Abuse." *Human Factors* 39, no. 2 (1997): 230-253.

Raji, Inioluwa Deborah, et al. "Closing the AI Accountability Gap: Defining an End-to-End Framework for Internal Algorithmic Auditing." *Proceedings of the 2020 Conference on Fairness, Accountability, and Transparency* (2020).

Selbst, Andrew D., et al. "Fairness and Abstraction in Sociotechnical Systems." *Proceedings of the Conference on Fairness, Accountability, and Transparency* (2019).

Reports and Other Sources

Angwin, Julia, et al. "Machine Bias." *ProPublica*, May 23, 2016.

Edelman Trust Barometer. Annual reports available at edelman.com.

Hao, Karen. "How Facebook got addicted to spreading misinformation." *MIT Technology Review*, March 11, 2021.

McKinsey & Company. "The State of AI." Annual reports.

Pew Research Center. Surveys on public trust in institutions.

Ribeiro, Manoel Horta, et al. "Auditing radicalization pathways on YouTube." *Proceedings of the ACM Conference on Fairness, Accountability, and Transparency* (2020).

Stanford University Human-Centered Artificial Intelligence. *AI Index Report*. Annual reports.

ABOUT THE AUTHOR

Matthew Isabella is a high-stakes decision advisor who works with business owners, founders, and leadership teams navigating critical moments of risk, power, and change.

Over the past two decades, he has studied how decisions are actually made — not in theory, but in real environments where pressure, consequence, and human behaviour collide. His work spans hundreds of businesses, boardroom dynamics, and the underlying patterns that shape judgment, bias, and outcomes.

His first book, *The Power of "Your" Choice*, explored the personal side of decision-making — why individuals make the choices they do. In *The Power of AI's Choice*, Matthew expands that lens, examining what happens when flawed human decision-making is scaled into systems, institutions, and artificial intelligence.

Drawing on behavioural science, real-world observation, and emerging AI thinking, his work focuses on one central idea: if we don't understand how we make decisions, we have no chance of building systems that make them well.

Matthew is known for his direct, pragmatic approach — challenging conventional thinking and cutting through noise, ego, and narrative to focus on what actually drives outcomes.

END

www.ingramcontent.com/pod-product-compliance
Lightning Source LLC
Chambersburg PA
CBHW071104240526
45469CB00006BD/2326